# EXOTIC BIRDS

# EXOTIC BIRDS

DENNIS PAULSON

THE IMAGE BANK®

111 Fifth Avenue New York NY 10003

ISBN 0-941267-04-0

For rights information about the photographs in
this book please contact:

The Image Bank
111 Fifth Avenue, New York, N.Y. 10003

Printed and bound in Singapore

*Author:* Dennis Paulson

*Producer:* Robert M. Tod
*Managing Editor:* Elizabeth Loonan
*Designer and Art Director:* Mark Weinberg
*Editor:* Madelyn Larsen
*Production Coordinator:* Ann-Louise Lipman
*Picture Researcher:* Edward Douglas

*The green woodpecker is a common enough bird; but I had never seen one close. Here I saw every striking detail: the rich green of the wings, the flash of bright yellow on the back when he flew, the pale glittering eye, the scarlet nape, the strange moustache of black and red: and the effect was if I had seen a bird of paradise, even a phoenix.*

—Sir Julian Huxley

# Preface

These beautiful photographs have brought into focus unusual birds from far-flung parts of the world, most of them exotic in every sense of the word. Yet to preface this collection of special birds, I wish to make the point that *all* birds are among the most interesting beings with which we share our planet. Some have such slender, long-winged aerial grace as to generate almost religious awe in those of us who are earthbound. It is surely their mastery of the air that kindles our admiration, even our outright envy. Thus the purpose of these brief remarks is to share my admiration of birds and bird life with anyone whose eye has been captured by these exotic visual images.

## Why Exotic Birds?

With the commonplace not only interesting but often surpassingly beautiful, why should the exotic fascinate us so? The two primary definitions of exotic—"of foreign origin or character" and "something unusual or strange"— make this clear: it is *unfamiliar*.

As much as anything I can envision, birds are exotic. On the most elementary level, everything about birds invokes a sense of the exotic: their colors, their sounds, their mastery of the air, ultimately their amazing variety. They are the most unusual among the familiar objects in our lives. When we go beyond the superficial to scrutinize sexual behavior, try to understand feeding adaptations or go with migrant flocks as they launch over the ocean, then we uncover a deeper, even more exotic layer. Something must attract our attention, or else why would there be so many birdwatchers?

## More Than 57 Varieties

With almost 9,000 species worldwide, birds present us with a diversity beyond contemplation. We have no way to take a mental inventory of all these birds, short of memorizing a rather dry list of species. No diverse tropical rain forest supports them all, no museum collection of neatly stuffed specimens is comprehensive, and no book comes even close to illustrating all varieties.

To see all birds in nature you would have to go *everywhere*, as many little oceanic islands support species found nowhere else. The person who has seen more bird species than anyone else in the world, a Canadian with suffficient free time and financial resources, has encountered somewhat over 6,100 of them, and only a tiny number of equally persistent birdwatchers have seen even half the species.

A book with color plates of all the birds of the world would be worth almost any amount paid for it. With a few paragraphs about each species and a range map showing its distribution, it would be one of the world's great books. In order to provide details of all plumages, including variation by age, sex, geographic region, and season and, of course, to illustrate them in flight, no more than two species could be shown per plate. This "book" would consist of twenty volumes of over 200 plates each and would be a life's work for any artist indomitable enough to attempt it.

The present volume barely touches on this diversity. It is more as if an expedition from outer space visited the earth to learn all it could about us but had only a weekend during which to do it. At the very least, I hope the reader will have an educational and enjoyable weekend!

Bird diversity is much higher in the tropics than in temperate regions because the long climatic stability of tropical latitudes has permitted great specialization by birds on specific components of the food resources that are available and very specific ways to acquire them. Thus any treatment of unusual birds has to pay close attention to the great tropical avifauna, and the majority of the photographs in this book are of tropical birds.

The New World tropics support the highest bird diversity of anywhere in the world. Because they are large countries, because they lie on or near the Equator, and because of the complexity of their mountain systems, Colombia with 1,695 and Peru with 1,678 species are the record holders. With continued field work, new species are being added to the lists of these contries every year. In fact, most of the last few dozen newly described bird species were discovered in Peru.

## Variations on a Theme

All birds are basically similar, constrained by aspects of their life such as flight (the ancestral bird was a flying object) and reproduction (all birds lay eggs). Nevertheless, there are many variations on this theme. The smallest bird is the Bee Hummingbird of Cuba, weighing as much as one of the pennies in your pocket. This mote—a bird in every way though not much larger than its namesake—could perch scarcely noticed on your ear, although it would certainly tickle, being excessively active.

The largest living is the African Ostrich, almost 70,000 times heavier than the hummer and much too large to be airborne.

# Aerial Adaptations

All birds—but no other animals—have feathers, and those feathers neatly arranged in wings and tails that allow the birds to fly above the domain of earthbound creatures, are what make them so special. The shapes of their wings and their tails determine what sorts of aerial creatures they are.

An American Robin has a pair of average bird wings, sufficient to get it from place to place in its daily life. Its wings carry it between a nesting or roosting tree and feeding sites, provide it with rapid burst of speed to chase off a territorial intruder or to escape a pursuing hawk, and, strongly and steadily beating, carry it high in the air to migrate hundreds of miles between summer and winter homes.

The sky, however, only temporarily invaded by robins, belongs to the large-winged birds. These birds come in two types: with long, narrow, pointed wings for gliding and long-distance flight, and with long, broad, rounded wings for extended soaring.

## Long-winged Birds

Swallows and swifts are insect-searchers, covering dozens and even hundreds of miles each day over forest, fields, and lakes. Wherever their prey swarm, these little flying machines will find them. Swifts, with their very long, narrow wings, are so highly adapted for flight and so poorly adapted for perching that they are able both to sleep and to mate on the wing—the only birds to do so. They do come to earth to nest, however; no bird has shed this basic link to its egg-laying reptilian ancestors.

The other long-winged birds are seabirds, most of which must be distance flyers to locate the erratic fish schools on which they depend for a living. The wing of an albatross is five to six times as long as it is wide, shaped much like an arm but of course flattened from top to bottom (one of many reasons why birds can fly and we can't). Albatrosses, gulls, shearwaters, and other birds of this type can glide into a light wind with never a flap, using the earth's own air movement to support them in their incessant search pattern. Fortunatly, gull are sufficiently common and widespread that anyone can see this superb flight style in action.

The frigatebirds of tropical latitudes are more extreme yet; their wings are almost *too* long, their bodies too light. They would be blown away in temperate-zone oceans where heavier shearwaters and albatrosses body surf on the gusting winds. But their long wings and long, forked tail give them total control of the air, fitting them for life as avian pirates.

Frigatebirds are kleptoparasites, forcibly appropriating fish from other birds that have captured them. They chase boobies and terns impartially, by their large size, aggressive pursuit, and sheer flying skill almost always forcing their victim to drop its fish, which they catch in midair and quickly swallow. Some other predatory birds such as gulls and hawks attempt similar pursuits, but only the jaegers and skuas, close relatives of the gulls, are as successful as the frigates.

Spectacular as frigatebird chases are, they are outclassed by those of jaegers, which can fly rings around the most agile tern. A jaeger that sees a small gull or tern capture a fish accelerates from cruising speed to nail its victim instantly or to pursue it through a series of increasingly frantic evasive actions. If the fish is not dropped quickly enough, the jaeger may grab a wing or tail and whirl the smaller bird in the air, with predictable outcome. The longest of these chases last for many seconds and cover wide airspaces, with the thrill of a World War I dogfight.

## Broad-winged Birds

The other sky masters are the soaring birds: hawks, eagles, and vultures that hunt from the sky and pelicans, cranes, and storks that move cross-country by the same air currents. These birds all have expansive wings, both long and relatively broad, to take advantage of air currents that go up rather than sideways. Thermals are produced as the earth is heated and the hot air just above it rises, and these big birds ride thm upward, most of them not taking to the air until midmorning.

A thermal is merely an aerial perch for a hunting hawk, a way to hang in the air with minimal expenditure of energy. From high above, a hawk, with vision far sharper than our own, can distinguish a mouse or grasshopper twitch from the waving of the grass around it, drop out of the sky, and snatch it up in one smooth gesture or, spreading those broad wings, stop instantly to readjust at any height before its final stoop.

At the other extreme are the accelerator birds, species that specialize in quick bursts of speed to capture fleeting prey or even quicker bursts—a matter of life or death rather than a meal gained or lost—to escape their predators. Both bird-eating hawks and hawk-eaten birds, in particular members of the grouse and pheasant family, have short, strongly rounded wings for rapid takeoff. The grouse and their relatives have very stiff, curved wing feathers, with which they leave the ground or tree branch like a rocket, often with a burst of wing sound that startles the flusher into distraction.

## Tails

Tails are not always necessary accoutrements, as some birds virtually lack them. But they are prominent parts of the anatomy of most birds, as they provide first-rate flight-control surfaces. The more agile a bird is in flight, the more likely it is to have a lengthy tail. Look at a Barn Swallow or a Common Tern to see how the long, forked tail is used. The frigatebird's maneuverability is in part a consequence of its magnificent tail.

The fact that so many conspicuous markings occur on tails indicates their value as signaling devices. The white edges and tips of the tails of some small flocking birds suddenly appear when a bird flies, signaling to other members of the flock that a predator has been seen or that it is time to move on. Such signals may serve the additional important function of informing a potential predator that it has been seen by an alert pair of eyes, making a capture attempt futile. Fanned, depressed, elevated, even waved back and forth, a tail can also express the varying moods of its owner.

A very long tail is a hindrance in flight to some birds, but such tails have been elaborated as display ornaments. Macaws and other long-tailed parrots almost invariably have bright colors on their tails. Birds of paradise and their namesakes, the paradise flycatchers, have greatly lengthened central tail feathers; while in the Scissor-tailed Flycatcher and in many hummingbirds, such as comets and sylphs, it is the outer feathers that are lengthened and, in most cases, strikingly beautiful. In motmots, part of the the web of each central tail feather deteriorates and is picked off, leaving a racket tip; the tail is unmistakably that of a motmot when swung back and forth in metronome fashion.

In quetzals and peafowl, the uppertail coverts have become lengthened for display, but in the Crested Argus Pheasant the tail itself—at almost six feet, the longest of any bird—forms a peacocklike display.

## Getting Around on the Ground

Every bird has two legs to stand on, but some of them stand less than others. Swifts, with their short, weak legs, come to earth only to hang on the sides of cliffs, caves, and chimneys; otherwise, they remain in the air. At the other extreme are the long-legged waders and the strong-legged runners.

Cranes and herons, although superficially similar, use their long legs somewhat differently. Cranes advance rapidly over open ground in search of the small animals on which they prey, some species stopping at intervals to dig in the ground for tubers. Rapid walking is also practiced by other long-legged birds, such as the Secretarybird in Africa—a snake-eating hawk—and the seriemas of South America that are the hawk's equivalent on that continent. Herons wade in water deep enough to ensure an abundant supply of fish, and wading is also the way of life for other heron relatives such as storks and ibises and for many shorebirds such as yellowlegs and stilts.

While some birds walk, others run. Many birds of prairie and beach habitats are runners, and again shorebirds are good examples of this means of locomotion. The Sanderlings racing the waves up and down the ocean beach are modified for running in the same way the huge Ostriches and Emus are: they lack a hind toe, which has no function in a running bird and might even get in the way. Ostriches may not be able to fly, but with only two toes, like the antelopes with which they associate, they glide across the plains at 40 miles per hour, a higher speed than may birds attain in normal flight.

## Exotic Utensils and Diets

Just as wing and tail shapes tell the story of the flight styles of birds, bill shapes tell the story of what they eat and how they get it. Bills are amazing appendages, the primary feeding tools of birds and comparable to our hands rather than our noses. No bird would envy us our paltry array of knives, forks, and spoons at the dinner table; at minimum we would have to add from the kitchen cabinet nutcrackers, straws, strainers, and chopsticks to be their equals.

Bird bills vary from short, slender, insect-picking forceps and sturdy seed crackers to the stabbing daggers of large herons, the fishing scoops of pelicans, and the upside-down shrimp strainers of flamingos. Some of them, like the brightly plated bills of puffins, seem bizarre only until we realize that they are also used for display, their feeding prowess undiminished by their seeming awkwardness.

### Fishing Birds

From the great variety of fishing birds, it is obvious that there are many ways to skin a catfish. Many fishing birds are spear bearers, their bills long, straight, and sharply pointed to spear or to dart through the water for quick capture. Herons, egrets, and anhingas sneak up on their prey, the anhingas beneath the surface and the others while wading. Loons, grebes, and other diving birds pursue fish rapidly underwater. The flashiest examples of this feeding strategy are the penguins, which can outswim any fish in the sea.

Storks and cranes have bills something like those of herons but more versatile. The huge Saddlebill Storks of Africa have awesome bills, used for capturing almost anything that moves. Snakes, baby birds, and rats are quite acceptable any time they cross the path of a stork looking for fish or frogs.

Cormorants have strong hooks on the ends of their bills for a tight grasp on a squirming fish. They bring their prey to the surface, manipulate it for a while and then swallow it. The long bills of frigatebirds are very strongly hooked and look like wicked and very effective weapons. As these highly aerial birds try to stay dry-feathered while capturing their fish from the surface, they have to be good!

Many fishing birds search for prey from the air. Gulls drop to the surface, often submerging a few inches; but terns dive from higher up, briefly disappearing underwater and coming up with a fish firmly grasped in their long, pointed bills. After a good shake to get rid of excess water from their feather, they flip the fish to point it in the right direction for swallowing or carrying back to the nest.

Ospreys and sea eagles soar over lakes and bays and drop on surface fish with talons outstretched. The value of their large wings is obvious after a successful capture, as they beat strongly along the surface and finally become airborne with a fish that may weigh almost as much as the bird.

Pelicans are indeed funny birds. Whether Brown Pelicans diving from the air or White Pelicans swimming across the surface in groups, they seem to do everything with deliberation. Their deliberations must work, as they come up with fish in their expansive pouches at a sufficient rate to keep them alive.

It isn't easy to be a fishing bird. In all species that have been studied, adults are more successful than their young in catching fish, and young birds must mature for some years—often four or five—before they are competent to raise their own families. Anyone fortunate enough to see flocks of Brown Pelicans feeding can observe this difference between clumsy youngsters and accomplished adults.

## Shorebirds

Probing in the mud is somewhat easier than fishing, and sandpipers typically mature in two years. Their bills vary from quite short, for picking insects from the surface, to long and slender, for deep probing in mud and water. Sandpipers have sensitive nerve endings in the bill tip, and they feel each wiggling creature they contact and snatch it up with scarcely a pause in their sewing-machinelike probing.

Some sandpipers have ridiculously long bills, and a Long-billed Curlew looks as if it could prop its head up any time it wished to take a break. But with this bill, curlews are equally able to take insect larvae from among the grasses of their breeding grounds or small crabs from their burrows on the mud flats where they winter.

Other shorebirds, such as avocets, have upcurved bills. They feed by sweeping their bills rapidly through the shallow water of alkaline lakes, grabbing tiny crustaceans and fish in rapid succession. Unrelated, and with quite different bills, the much larger spoonbills feed in similar fashion.

Ibises, closely related to spoonbills, have bills like curlews—including the sensitive nerves on the tip—and feed somewhat like them, although they probe deeply for invisible prey even more. It is fascinating that ibises and spoonbills have such different bills. How could an ibis bill be modified into that of a spoonbill or vice versa over evolutionary time? Or what was their straight-billed ancestor like? Nothing in the fossil record to date allows us to answer these questions.

## Insect-eaters

Breaking away from the large and showy species for a moment, what do all the little birds that we see around our houses eat? Most of them eat the two foods that are most abundant in nature; insects and seeds. There are more species of insects than all the other animals put together, and the number of individual insects is beyond estimate. As there are so many, they furnish a very important food source for small animals of all kinds, including birds.

Perhaps as many as half of the living bird species are insect-eaters, with familiar species including chickadees, wrens, warblers, swallows, and thrushes. The basic insect-eater moves continually through the leaves and twigs and takes its prey with a bill modifies into a pair of fine forceps. The larger the prey, the larger the bill, and the prey of the largest-billed birds are large enough to be rather uncommon. Species such as trogons, motmots, rollers, and kookaburras that eat very large insects for example, sit quietly and watch for them. then make a sudden dart through the air.

Other insect-eaters are aerially oriented, such as bee-eaters with long, pointed wings for rapid flight and long, narrow bills to grab a bee, wasp, or dragonfly right out of the air by its wings.

Bee-eaters and flycatchers hunt flying insects from perches, but swallows and swifts hunt them from the air, circling high above the countryside to scoop up tiny flies, beetles, and moths with their broad, short bills.

Other birds are specialized for taking insects from tree trunks. Nuthatches and creepers pick their prey from the bark surface and crevices, while woodpeckers bore directly into the bark for juicy beetle larvae that they detect by the sounds the larvae make moving in their tunnels. Woodpecker Finches go one step further, picking up cactus spines to poke into crevices to dislodge otherwise inaccessible insects. Tool-using like this is rare in the avian world and thus is especially noteworthy.

### Seed-eaters

Seeds are similarly superabundant in the natural world, and may birds have evolved adaptations to deal with them. Doves and blackbirds swallow seeds in great quantities and crush them in their muscular gizzards to extract their highly nutritive contents. To assist in the grinding process, they also swallow small stones that remain for a short while in the gizzard. Many of the birds you see at the roadside in the early morning or late afternoon are there to pick up a fresh supply of gizzard stones, and one wonders what they did before there were highways.

Seeds persist through the northern winter, whereas most insects disappear from the surface. Most of the birds that similarly disappear from the North at this time are insect-eaters, and most of the ones that stay behind are seed-eaters, the birds that visit bird feeders so avidly during cold weather. In fact, some species have greatly expanded their winter distributions because so many Americans feed birds. The insect-eaters that remain include woodpeckers that take larvae from within the bark and chickadees that forage on insect eggs from the lower surfaces of leaves.

### Fruit-eaters

Although it helps a plant in no way if its seeds are eaten by a bird, many plants *are* helped by the food habits of birds. The fleshy fruits produced by plants are wonders of packaging, each one a brightly colored container to catch the attention of a wandering bird and each full of sugar to make it both edible and nourishing. Within these attractive fruits are seeds that pass through the bird's digestive tract and are defecated at a distance from the parent plant, assuring dissemination of the offsping of an organism that has no way of distributing them itself.

We should be thankful that, besides having so many other attributes that we admire, birds are such mobile creatures that they furnish the best way for some plants to disperse their seeds. Only because of this interaction, favorable for both plant and bird, do cherries, strawberries, blueberries, grapes, and most of our favorite fruits exist. Temperate-zone birds are not obligate fruit-eaters but, like us, take fruit as a seasonal part of their diets. Examples include robins and other thrushes, waxwings, and starlings. Most fruits are not nutritious enough to serve as a complete diet, and most fruit-eating birds feed insects to their growing young.

However, fruit-eating is a much more serious business in the tropics, where birds can depend on the year-round availability of fruits. Many trees have large, fleshy, oily fruits that are quite nutritive and constitute the only food of certain birds. Fruit specialists include cotingas, birds of paradise, oilbirds, barbets, turacos, and fruit pigeons, most of them considerably larger than our familiar fruit-eating birds.

Some other fruit-eaters specialize very narrowly; for example, some eat only mistletoe berries. The small tanagers and flowerpeckers that eat these fruits do their own "kissing under the mistletoe." They wipe off the sticky remnants adhering to their bills on branches, thereby spreading mistletoe seeds throughout the treetops.

### Nectar-eaters

Another such interaction concerns an additional part that the plant can spare, its energy-rich nectar. Flowers produce abundant nectar to attract animals to visit them repeatedly. The animals in turn visit other flowers and transfer pollen in that manner, assuring the plants' reproduction. By specializing on one type of pollinator, the plant assures that its pollen is transferred to others of its own species. This has brought about mutual adaptations among plants and their pollinators, such as close correspondence in flower length and bill length.

Northern latitudes are not rich in bird-pollinated flowers, but in the stable tropics such interactions are commonplace. Hummingbirds are all nectar-feeders, as are the sunbirds of Africa and the honeyeaters of Australia. All have bills and tongues modified for taking nectar, and most are small bo be able to perch on the flowers or to hover in front of them to feed. Most flowers visited by nectar-feeding birds are tubular, and many of them are red—not because birds need flowers of that shape and color but because most insects, potentially severe competitors for this limited resource, cannot detect red and cannot reach into long, tubular flowers.

### Leaf-eaters

Leaves which are not very nutritious and are difficult to digest, are eaten by few birds, but certain groups are especially adapted to handle them. Geese and grouse are the primary grazers and browsers of the bird world, with long intestines to pack in a lot of leaves and a rather sedate life style compared with many other birds. Their diets makes them rather tasty, and geese are large, live in the open, and stay in flocks, all of which are effective ways of avoiding predators. Grouse are among the best-camouflaged of birds, sitting quietly and almost invisibly as they snip off leaves from around them.

### A More Unusual Diet

Some bird diets are more exotic than others. How many people realize how difficult it is to be a vulture? A carrion-eating bird has to get a carcass quickly, as it is competing with the much more numerous insects and bacteria. Carrion-eaters have no special adaptations other than naked heads to avoid matting of their feathers and the ability to search wide areas from the air. The Turkey Vulture is, in addition, provided with an excellent sense of smell for finding squirrel-sized carcasses in wooded country; no one knows if they also can detect a flower in bloom.

A flying bird quarters the wind, often low over the ground, and follows its nostrils upwind as soon as a meal is detected. Black Vultures soar high above and watch for any of their kind— or, more likely, a Turkey Vulture—to drop from the sky, immediately converging on the spot. The aggresive Blacks can displace the first-arriving Turkeys from a carcass and in turn are themselves displaced by the larger, rarer King Vultures.

The vulture hierarchy is even more complex in East Africa, where six species may converge on a lion kill. The low-flying White-headed and Lappet-faced vultures arrive first, able to tear meat from the carcass and keep the other species at bay with their large bills. Ruppell's Griffons and especially White-backed Vultures overwhelm their larger relatives by their very numbers, their long necks allowing them to poke well inside the banquet. The much smaller Egyptian and Hooded vultures hang around the perimeter and take what they can get from the leavings. Finally, a few gangly Marabou Storks will be present at certain of these feasts, pursuing their own vulturine diet.

# All the Colors of the Rainbow

Birds come in every familiar color and some that have to be seen to be believed. We are fortunate to have evolved color vision, so we can see birds as they see each other. Their colors have delighted observers and artists for generations, but the functions of all these different colors are scarcely understood. In part this is because variations on color themes and schemes seem almost endless.

One study of perching birds of North and Central America found brown to be the most common overall color, followed by gray, black, and green. Deep in tropic Panama, only 10 percent of the birds were predominantly brightly colored, while, surprisingly, in nothern areas there was a slightly higher percentage of colorful birds. Of course, as there are many more bird species in tropical areas, there are also more highly colored ones in the tropics. Yellow and blue are the next most common colors, with red far down the list, prominent on fewer than one percent of the species.

Anyone visiting Central or South America is struck by the procession of gaudy red or blue tanagers, orange orioles, and yellow flycatchers flying across a country lane, each eliciting a gasp as it appears briefly in the early morning sun. What you don't see on such an excursion are all the little brown birds that remain within the thickets, far more kinds than in any northern woodland. So no matter where you go, dull birds are the norm and bright ones *should* be appreciated.

Birds with pure swatches of bright color are especially satisfying to those of us with simple tastes. When the bird is one color head to tail, we can think about its shape or size or flight calls or merely its pure beauty without being diverted by details such as eyerings, malar stripes, wing bars, or undertail coverts.

### Red, Orange and Pink Birds

Red birds probably garner more admiration than those of most other colors. Red stands for hear and fire; it ignites our passions. A male Vermilion Flycatcher on a fence wire in Mexico or Venezuela will stop me with screeching brakes every time. And there is nothing like a Scarlet Tanager against the light-green spring growth in a New England woodlot, except perhaps five of them in one tree after a fallout of spring migrants on the Louisiana coast. Red contrasts so vividly with green leaves that I wonder why there aren't many more red birds; but I suppose when all things are considered, there are just enough of them.

Like any other color, red can be flaunted or hidden. Birds

with "crowned" in their names are usually examples of color best appreciate at close range. The Ruby-crowned Kinglet is a mite of a bird, common in northern North American woodlands but barely evident much of the time. Yet when spring rolls around, the male feels the urge to sing, his hidden crown patch flares, the bush lights up like a four-alarm fire, and all attention focuses on this bird, transformed for the moment. The fire lasts for seconds; the observer is transformed forever.

Among birds more orange than red, male cocks-of-the-rock of South American jungles are brilliantly showy, and it is amazing that one, perched silently, can disappear into that same foliage with which it contrasts so much. In fact, it is probably well hidden when in a dense tangle of leaves and branches, but when it flies from tree to tree it does so in a burst of color. Fortunately, predatory birds are sufficiently uncommon that the risk of being so conspicuous does not exceed the benefits. A group of males in display must be irresistable to any female in the area.

Pink brings to mind flamingos, and, indeed, these are the birds most prominently endowed with this color. However, only the American Flamingo is truly brilliant, and it shows not a trace of pink. Most of the six flamingo species, in fact, feature other colors such as white or red, and none looks exactly like the classic lawn ornament. Roseate Spoonbills have as much pink on them as any bird, although a Pink Cockatoo at close range is equally impressive.

The bright colors of flamingos come in large part from the tiny crustaceans, containing red carotenoid pigments, that make up their diet. Before this was known, flamingos in zoos, no matter how they flourished, became paler and paler, eliciting considerable concern on the part of their keepers. With enlightenment came the solution, a diet supplement of carrot juice!

### Blue Birds

My favorite birds are blue, my favorite color. Fortunately, they appear on every continent. Ohio has its Blue Jay, Eastern Bluebird, Blue-gray Gnatcatcher, Black-throated Blue Warbler, Cerulean Warbler, Blue Grosbeak, and Indigo Bunting, just as Trinidad has its Blue Ground-Dove, Blue-and-yellow Macaw, Blue-headed Parrot, Blue-chinned Sapphire, Blue-tailed Emerald, Blue-crowned Motmot, Blue-and-white Swallow, Blue Dacnis, and Turquoise, Blue-gray, and Blue-capped tanagers. Little Blue Herons and Blue-winged Teals occur in both places.

Some "blue" birds aren't. Blue-black Grassquits look black to me, and Great Blue Herons are only a shade blue of gray.

Conversely, birds are blue with no hint of it in their names. Look at the iridescent blues in two of our familiar birds, the ultramarine Barn Swallow and the viridian Tree Swallow.

Most of us know that blue is not a pigment but a structural color. The microstructure of a blue bird's feather is such that only blue light is reflected, while all other wavelengths pass through—are they lost forever? Thus blue birds are more or less blue, lighter or darker, depending on the angle of the light source from the viewer. They can even look black—the absence of reflected light—in the shadows.

## Green Birds

A green feather is a yellow feather with blue bird structure, except in turacos, with their unique green pigments. Many green birds have brightly colored patches on their heads, wings, or tails for close-range display. Many green parrots have bright red patches on their wings, visible only when they take off. Parrots are essentially invisible when perched quietly in a forest tree, but their red patches are available when needed. Unlike a stoplight, this flash of color signals "go," and all parrots in the tree collect into a flock, streak off through the forest, and vanish once again as they land in another tree.

These birds of tropical forests are not seen when they don't choose to be. Migratory birds of temperate-zone forests for some reason are quite different—drab olive-green or olive-brown above and gray to white below, this much duller look apparently just right for both their breeding habitats and the tropical woodlands in which they winter.

### Iridescent Birds

Iridescence, like blue, is in the eye of the beholder. It seems primarily to have evolved so that black birds can, at times, be dazzlingly bright. The introduced and unloved Eurasian Starlings, so common in our cities now, are as good examples an any of this phenomenon; although simply described as "black," a spring male shines green and purple in the sun. It fades to insignificance, however, in the company of African relatives the names of which portray a hint of their brilliance: Superb Starling, Violet-backed Starling, Bronze-tailed Starling, and Splendid Glossy Starling. For some reason, Africa seems especially favorable for iridescent birds.

North America is not as rich in iridescent birds, but our grackles do their part to stand in for the considerably gaudier African starlings. South America has more of them, mostly restricted to a few small groups like the trogons, jacamars, kingfishers, and certain tanagers, but the hummingbirds of that continent are as iridescent as any birds in the world.

Hummingbirds have more iridescent colors on them than perhaps all other birds put together. Some of them are iridescent, usually green, all over. Many of them have iridescent patches on the throat, breast, or crown, often cotnrasting with the body color and each other. This diversity is well served by the English names that have been given these avian gems—Shining Sunbeam, Empress Brilliant, Velvet-purple Coronet, Golden-bellied Starfrontlet, Glittering-throated Emerald, and Purple-crowned Fairy are a few examples among many.

### Multicolored Birds

How many colors can be painted onto one bird? There must be a maximum, and it is exemplified by the male Golden Pheasant, almost unbelievable with its yellow, light and dark orange, red, iridescent green and blue, black, dark and light brown, and pale buff. One wonders why purple and pure white are lacking. The runner-up is a very different bird of the marshes of southern South America, the *siete colores*, or Many-colored Rush-Tyrant, which the usually steadfast Charles Darwin called "an exquisitely beautiful little bird." Black and white, blue and green, red, orange, and yellow are all plainly visible on both sexes of this otherwise undistinguished little bird.

Only a few New Guinea fruit-doves equal the seven colors of the rush-tyrant, and they are primarily green, with patches of additional colors. The Blue-winged Pitta of southeast Asia has six vividly distinct colors, and other pittas are equally varied. So are some of the parrots and lorikeets of Australia and New Guinea. Among the tanagers, many of them breathtakingly brilliant, five colors seems to be the limit in the Multicolored and Paradise varieties.

# Black and White Birds

White and black are common seabird colors. Being white makes birds more conspicuous from a distance and facilitates the social behavior so common among them. Most seabirds nest in colonies and many of them forage in groups, the individuals in the group benefit by the group effort.

White species of pelicans often feed in flocks, swimming in a line in shallow water to drive schools of fish ahead of them for easier capture. Some cormorants and mergansers do the same. Feeding interactions of seabirds become complex in some areas, where gulls dive on fish schools from above and cormorants and auklets attack them from below. The white plumage of the first gull that dives on such a school surely serves as a beacon to attract the other member of the gang.

White Ibises feed in groups, moving rapidly through shallow water as they probe for little creatures in the mud. Both egrets and herons are attracted to these groups and to each other and are often able to capture fish startled by advancing ibises or wading egrets. Researchers have shown that models of white egrets attract other egrets and herons much more than do similar, darkly colored models.

Interestingly, the most common variation of the white-bird theme is red, orange, and pink. These colors, perhaps easily produced by birds that eat the shrimps that are so rich in red pigments, are found on ibises, storks, spoonbills, and flamingos, all long-legged wading birds that come together in groups to nest and feed.

Many seabirds are black—perhaps also a social color, as quite a few land birds that form flocks are also black. Blackbirds and starlings from the largest flocks, in fact, and a single flock moving through the air as a unit may contain many hundreds of birds and a roost where they all assemble, many hundreds of thousands. Estimates of five million Red-winged Blackbirds are about the largest counts of single bird species at one place in North America, although Bramblings, small finches of Eurasia, have been estimated in similar numbers. Imagine the seeds it would take to feed this congregation over a winter's time!

The highly social crows and ravens are black, visible for long distances as they fly over green forests and farmlands. The importance of color, or at least predictability, to birds is evident any time an oddly colored individual appears. Albinistic or partially albinistic crows are usually driven from their flocks, with little chance to mate and transmit their aberrant genes to the next generation. Yet a few species of crows and ravens are adorned with conspicuous white markings.

Many black-and-white birds are strikingly patterned, deserving a place in anyone's list of unusual birds. Somehow this crisp patterning puts them in a special category. Magpies, both in the northern hemisphere and in Australia, are particularly vivid. Would penguins be such dependable subjects for cartoons if they were dressed less formally? There are no entirely black penguins, but water birds of other groups, such as cormorants and puffins, have both black and black-and-white species. Perhaps both of these color schemes are equally effective at being conspicuous.

### Brown Birds — Are They Dull?

Some of the birds on our planet are endowed with patterns so complex they would confuse a computer programmer, yet these patterns blend into harmonious wholes that best fit them for existence in their particular world. Nature furnishes a complex background, and the most complexly colored birds are those that merge into this background rather than contrast with it as the brightly colored species do.

Familiar examples are our wrens and sparrows, basically brown and gray but streaked, spotted, and barred with all sorts of fine black markings. Some of them can be distinguished by birdwatchers only with difficulty, but presumably they can recognize each other perfectly well. One marvels at the evolutionary fine-tuning that has put streaks on the sparrows pipits of grassland environments and spots on the woodland-inhabiting thrushes.

These birds are camouflaged when sitting still; when for example, they are on their nest or when they "freeze" as a predator passes. But most of their daily activity involves moving actively about the environment as they forage to obtain enough food to stoke their inner metabolic fires. Therefore, they can be seen by potential predators even though in cryptic shades of brown. Perhaps this is why they are rather boring with regard to pattern complexity.

On the other hand, the birds that really benefit from being invisible are those that forage at night. Perching in one place throughout the daylight hours, they should match their background perfectly. Owls and nightjars are among the birds that do so. They are the most complexly patterned birds, with intricate designs on each feather that provide a continuity between bird and its surroundings to fool the most discerning predator. Screech-owls and certain other owls show this patterning, and it becomes obvious that it is a night-bird adaptation when one realizes that owls active in the daytime show no hint of it.

The nocturnally active woodcocks also show complex patterning, but it is developed to its extreme in the goatsuckers, or nightjars. Both names for members of this group are equally fascinating; none of them suckle from goats, as far as we know, but the loud calls of some species do jar the night. The Common Poorwill of the American West is one of those goatsuckers (or nightjars), and it has been called the most beautiful bird by one student of night birds. Any aficionado of subtle beauty fortunate enough to get a very close look at one might agree, but the even more poorly know pauraques, potoos, frogmouths, and owlet-

nightjars of other parts of the world would be equal competitors in such a beauty contest. No book illustration can do justice to these birds.

# The Familiar and the Exotic

Exotic, of course, is entirely in the eye of the beholder. A citizen of Manaus may think nothing of a flock of Scarlet Macaws flying over at dawn; this is as much a part of the day as breakfast. Similarly, a resident of Nairobi may see an Ostrich while commuting to the office, while a lucky New Yorker may see a Ruby-throated Hummingbird—a bird almost inconceivable to an African ornithologist—zip across the freeway. I grew up with Painted Buntings at by bird feeder in Miami, seldom wondering how startling such birds would be to anyone unfamiliar with them.

### South American Birds

Without doubt, South America is the bird continent. About 3,000 species occur there, fully one-third of all the birds of the world, and several hundred additional species occur in Central America and Mexico, also part of the great neotropical realm.

With the vast, somber forests of the Amazon basin, it is not surprising that a lot of the birds of South America are small and brown. The sedentary forest-dwelling ovenbirds and antbirds, entirely absent from temperate North America but two of South America's largest families, account for about 500 species. There are over 300 tyrant flycatchers, dominant in the tropics but able to perform long-distance flights; a few of them migrate north to Canada and Alaska. The only other really large groups are the 240 tanagers and 320 hummingbirds of South and Central America.

One wouldn't think of discussing South American birds without a word about hummingbirds. Although this American family reaches from southern Alaska to Tierra del Fuego, it is primarily a group of tropical latitudes. Perhaps its name is an oxymoron, but the Giant Hummingbird really *is* big, about the size of a small sparrow, and you can actually see its wings moving as it whirs past.

A single hummingbird occurs in the eastern United States and a few more occur in the West, but the diversity builds rapidly to the South. Fifty species inhabit Mexico, 51 are known from tiny Costa Rica, and Colombia's total is 143. A visit to a South American garden, with its profusion of bright flowers and buzz of hummingbird activity, is like no other experience.

Hummingbirds are insectlike in many ways, all of them

related to their nectar-feeding role. They are the smallest birds, their size appropriate to their need to spend time hovering at small flowers, along with the bees with which they compete. Hummingbirds' wings rotate 180 degrees on their axis, allowing them not only to hover but, unlike any other bird, to fly backwards. Their feeding apparatus has already been described, but the long tongue, rather like a bee's proboscis, must be mentioned. When it comes to colors, however, hummingbirds outshine most of the insect world.

The Purple-crowned Fairy is my favorite hummingbird, an acrylic in brilliant green and snowy white against the muted watercolors of the trees behind it; the male's purple crown seems an unnecessary touch. Literally sparkling as it hovers briefly in a patch of sunlight in a forest opening, the fairy flashes its long tail like a white semaphore. Each time I see one seems as if the first time.

## African Birds

Africa is made to order for birdwatchers, with not only an abundance of open country for good visibility but also plenty of trees scattered throughout it to provide perches for all kinds of exciting birds. Colorful bee-eaters, rollers, and kingfishers are common; birds of prey are amazingly diverse; and shrinking waterholes attract hordes of water birds of all kinds as the dry season ensues each year. Kenya's bird list stands at over a thousand species, more than in the United States and Canada combined.

Its dazzling array of gem-colored starlings and sunbirds make it clear that Africa, anything but a dark continent, is made to order for iridescence. Woodhoopoes, distinctly African, also glisten in the tropical sun. Even the swallows seem more iridescent than on other continents. Only the hummingbirds of the New World even approach the reflectivity of these African birds.

Africa is a dry, open continent compared with South America and tropical Asia. Just like our ape ancestors millions of years ago, many of the birds originally restricted to forests gave rise to open-country descendants. Only in Africa are there ground hornbills and a hawk that walks through the grass rather than flying. Open-country groups such as bustards, lapwings, starlings, shrikes, and larks are especially well-represented.

## Asian Birds

Japan, although not very large, has an impressive avifauna of over 500 species because it stretches over such a great latitudinal range. Birds have colonized this island nation from all along the Asian east coast, where there is a smooth transition from arctic tundra and boreal forest through temperate deciduous forest to subtropical and tropical evergreen forests. From the cranes that are almost symbolic of the country to the seven species of birds that occur nowhere else in the world but on its satellite islands, Japan is as worth visiting for its bird life as for its startling amalgam of ancient and modern culture.

The forests of the Southeast are rich in bird life, although less diverse than the South American tropics. Thailand has 850 species, an impressive list for a country smaller than Texas. Among them are fabulous birds—minivets, ground-cuckoos, pittas, huge hornbills, and tiny wren-babblers. The pittas alone are worth the visit, although, rainbow-bright as they are, they are just as difficult to see as their brown-and-rufous counterparts in South America, the ant-thrushes.

## Australian Birds

The continent down under is superb for exotic birds. So much of the countryside is open that its birds are visible, and what birds they are! Parrots are better represented, or at least certainly more obvious, than in other tropical areas. Australia's parrots are temperate-zone birds also, common right to the southern end of the continent at a latitude equivalent to that of San Francisco.

Although parrots are special birds in South America and Asia, birds of the jungle that must be sought diligently, they are so common in Australia that the average visitor sees them everywhere. In some years, it seems as if all the pet Budgerigars and Cockatiels in New York City apartments had teleported to Alice Springs. Photogenic beyond the fondest dreams of a local chamber of commerce, begging Crimson Rosellas adorn the shoulders of visitors to forest campgrounds throughout southeastern Australia.

Big, white Sulphur-crested Cockatoos with outrageous crests squawk through downtown parks: *escaped from a zoo,* one thinks, but no, this is where cockatoos come from! Rainbow Lorikeets screech rather than squawk as they blitz down the main streets of tropical towns like Cairns, descending on each flowering tree in turn in a flurry of pigment; if it were not for their constant vocalizations, watching the pointing tourists would be the way to find them.

Fairy wrens should be singled out as another exotic feature of the Australian bush. Its extremes of blueness defying description. The Splendid Wren of the Australian outback deserves it name, just as does its Superb relative that graces gardens in all the big cities. It's difficult to imagine small birds much brighter, and it comes as no surprise that these birds are not at all related to our northern wrens in their shades of brown.

Space doesn't permit adequate treatment of Australian birds, eclipsed perhaps only the glories of the New Guinea species; but the latter, primarily forest birds, are like forest birds everywhere: tough to see but easy to appreciate. The birds of paradise alone make it worth tramping through leech-infested forests, some of the males so gaudily colored and adorned as to invite speculation about what they could possibly do with all their ornamentation. But to watch one display is to see how all of these surrealistic feathers are put to admirable use indeed in the whirlwind competition for a mate that each male must undertake as the annual nesting season rolls around.

### Still Farther-out Birds

If distant lands are the home of exotic birds, we should survey the oceanic islands that are distant from just about everywhere. The Hawaiian Islands are as far from the mainland as any other island chain with well-developed bird communities. A quick perusal of any Hawaiian bird guide makes it clear that the islands are home to an extraordinary number of unusual birds.

Millennia ago, a wandering finch from the American mainland reached this mid-ocean archipelago, and over long periods of isolation, a diverse collection of birds evolved that included finchlike species with heavy, seed-cracking bills; insect eaters with short, pointed bills; and nectar-feeding species with long, even extremely long, slender bills. Like their finch relatives, they emphasized yellows and reds; and some species, such as the Ula-ai-hawane, Akohekohe, and Hawaii Mamo are particularly beautiful.

Anyone in search of distinctive birds will ultimately travel the distant parts of the earth—the Galapagos Islands, Madagascar, New Zealand, and even Antarctica. Most of Madagascar's long list of birds occur nowhere else in the world, and a visit to a colony of a hundred thousand Adélie Penguins in Antartica provides the visitor with unparalleled sights, sounds, and even smells.

### The Birds Right at Home

North America is—perhaps surprisingly, but perhaps not if one realizes where our birds originate—full of gaudy, strikingly colored birds. Most of them are migrants from tropical America,

where we expect to see such species. They include tanagers, warblers, orioles, and buntings, all groups with many bright representatives in the tropics.

## Bird Sounds

Birds are also special animals in our lives because we hear them so often. Imagine going outside and not hearing the call of a bird; birds are so ubiquitous that the term "silent spring" was coined to describe a world without life. The chirps of House Sparrows enrich the lives of city dwellers, and the crows that inhabit our countryside give us reason to rejoice in our bird life. But beyond these familiar sounds, listen for the symphony every spring when males of one species after another begin to sing. In some areas of rich bird diversity, the dawn chorus can almost be called deafening, with so many different voices that each part can be teased out of the whole only with some effort.

As a single example, the familiar Winter Wren, a tiny forest-floor inhabitant of northern North America, makes up in sound what it lacks in appearance. Its song has only recently been analyzed, and it is the most complex known bird song, loud enough to be heard over 500 yards away. In early spring a cascade of notes from each male issues from the otherwise-quiet conifer forest and hangs for moment in the air, surrounding the listener with sound as evocative as the aromatic verdancy of the forest itself.

## Exotic Lifestyles

Birds are not only variable in shape and coloration, but they exhibit an amazing array of behaviors, even to the level of variation among individuals in how they accomplish similar goals. Birds are not quite as stereotyped in their behavior patterns as we once believed just because their problem-solving abilities are different from those of mammals. Can you imagine learning what to eat and what not to eat from among the thousands of insects that might be encountered by a motmot in a Peruvian forest.

The nesting habits of birds represent as diverse an array of life styles as can be imagined. Most nests are made of twigs and grass, reaching their culmination in the huge nests of eagles, some of which would be large enough to suffice as a comfortable campsite for two. Stones and mud are common building materials for more permanent nests, and a major component of a solid penguin relationship is the constant furnishing of pebbles by each male to its mate. Large predators that can tear apart a stick nest have no chance against a bird that nests in a tree hole or rock crevice, and such brids often have large families and a leisurely growth period because of their relative safety.

Most small birds of temperate climates lay four or five eggs. Many seabirds, with the difficulties attendant on finding enough food in the open ocean, lay only a single egg; at the other extreme, some chickenlike birds fill up their nest with up to 15 eggs. Perhaps the most unusual nesting behavior involves the megapodes; males pile together mounds of soil and leaves wherein females deposit their eggs. The heat of the sun or rotting vegetation incubates the egg, and each male assiduously keeps track of its nest temperature, adding or subtracting nest material to regulate it. The eggs hatch into very advanced young, which can fly off into the underbrush only a day after they are born.

### Sexual Behavior

Unlike our own species, birds have not developed the attributes of shame, embarrassment, and modesty, so they carry out their sexual behavior in front of anyone as long as they don't feel threatened by a potential predator. The "act" is uncomplicated and no particular source of interest: males and females merely press their vents together long enough to transfer sperm—usually quickly enough that it might be missed altogether by an observer. In some groups of birds, the duct itself everts slightly to form a rudimentary copulatory organ.

It is in all of their many modes of pairing, however, that birds exemplify the exotic. These "mating systems" are of great interest to evolutionary biologists, as the proliferation of individual genes in offspring is such an important component of evolution. Most birds are straightforwardly monogamous, their mating systems as much like those of humans as can be in such different animals. A primary difference is found only in many migratory species, in which pairs form at the beginning of each breeding season and birds are as likely to be with a new mate as with the mate of the year before.

However, almost all tropical birds and many large migratory ones mate for life, pairing again only at the death of their mate. In species that separate for the nonbreeding season, both members of the pair return to the nest site well before the actual breeding season and renew their relationship by stereotyped courtship displays. It is not surprising that the displays need not be so vigorous toward a familiar mate as they are toward a new one.

"Faint heart never won fair lady" is an appropriate description of bird courtship, which is usually vigorous and prolonged. Those males that persist are the ones more likely to pass on their genes, and persistent types eventually become the norm. Thus there is a simple mechanistic explanation for the diversity and complexity of ways that male birds display to females, or both sexes display to each other, but in no way does the explanation diminish the excitement of seeing one of these displays performed.

Birds that make a living in the air usually have flight displays, perhaps to show off the aerial abilities that will be so important in capturing food for the young birds yet to come. Watch in open country in early spring for the dives and swoops, barrel rolls and loops of male birds of prey. Red-tailed Hawks and Golden Eagles fold their wings and dive steeply, then open them and ascend, in great roller-coaster paths through the sky. And pairs of Bald Eagles grasp talons in midair and drop toward the ground, wheeling round and round in a courtship dance as exhilarating as any polka; not bad for a national symbol.

Pairs of terns with mutual interest ascend ever higher, then swoop down in a beautifully coordinated *pas de deux* that elicits a gasp of wonderment from the human onlooker. At times I cannot decide whether to watch the birds, always thrilling, or the faces of first-time observers.

# Why Are Some Birds Rare?

Some birds are exotic just because of their rarity. Large birds have large territories because they have to roam over vast areas to get enough to eat. Thus there are relatively few of them, although even these birds at times come together in large numbers, as when over a thousand Bald Eagles descend on the Chilkat River of southern Alaska each winter to feed on the dead and dying salmon that have spawned there.

Birds of very limited distribution are also considered rare, but in fact they may be common where they occur. As the mobility of birds is well-known, it is surprising that a substantial number of species are restricted to single island groups or even single islands within archipelagos, such as the Hawaiian Islands. There are species found nowhere else in the world but on an island only a few miles wide. Recent studies of fossil birds from Pacific archipelagos, however, indicate that some of the restricted species may have been more widespread before human colonization of these islands. It seems that our own species is the greatest contributor to rarity in birds.

The Red-cockaded Woodpecker was a familiar bird to me in Florida two decades ago, but it has become alarmingly rare because of logging practices in its pinewoods habitat. Consequently, few beginning bird watchers have seen the species, which must be specially sought in fewer and fewer places. On the lsit of nationally endangered species, this bird now qualifies for government-funded research, symposiums, and habitat management and, on the down side, occasional destruction by loggers not wanting their forest patches protected.

Rare birds of our own continent include some truly magnificent species. Some—the Passenger Pigeon, Carolina Parakeet, and Ivory-billed Woodpecker—are already gone. Others—the California Condor, Aplomado Falcon, and Thick-billed Parrot—no longer fly over U.S. soil, but programs to release captive-bred birds are underway. In comparison, the Whooping Crane is a minor success story, with over 160 individuals in the wild from a former low of 15 in 1941, attributable to tremendous efforts on the part of conservationists. With a slow reproductive rate, these impressive white birds are recovering only slowly but they are recovering just the same.

Unfortunately, rare birds are just as common on other continents and much more so on islands, where their small populations and inability to cope with introduced predators and diseases make them extremely vulnerable to human effects. The Hawaiian Islands furnish a well-known example; the birds of these islands suffered two great extinctions: first, when the Polynesians reached them about 1,600 years ago, and second, soon after westerners arrived about 200 years ago. The Polynesians probably ate most of the larger birds and cut down enough of the lowland forests to extirpate many of the lowland species. The second wave of immigrants reduced the remaining upland forest cover and introduced mosquitoes carrying avian malaria, which further decimated lowland bird populations.

### The Future

So far, relatively few of the known bird species are extinct, and we are now beginning to realize how important birds and all other living things are to our own well-being. A planet treated with care will care for us in turn, and birds both exotic and familiar will continue to display their colors and sing their songs for our children and our children's children.

The magnificent Great Blue Heron (Ardea herodias) is common in freshwater marshes and on coastal mud flats all over North America. It nests in colonies that range from a few pairs to dozens of birds in forests and tree groves.

25

*Black-crowned Night-Herons (Nycticorax nycticorax) fly from*
*their roosts and spend the night fishing while other herons are asleep.*
*Their very large eyes fit them for this nocturnal way of life.*

Their long necks, long bills, and long legs adapt herons superbly for their way of life. They can stand still for minutes in shallow water, waiting for a fish to move near enough to capture with a thrust of the long neck.

Most birds spend the night asleep in a tree. Generally speaking, they are safe from predators that are active at that time. Their body weight locks tendons in their legs that hold them firmly on their perch.

*The Little Blue Heron (Egretta caerulea) has an unusual plumage change: the immature is white for about two years, looking much like an egret, then becomes cobalt-blue and maroon as an adult.*

*The legs of the Tricolored Heron (Egretta tricolor) are normally blue-gray but turn red for a few days just at the height of mating. The ornamental plumes are fully developed throughout the period of courtship and mating.*

*The Tricolored Heron was long called a Louisiana Heron, but the names of many birds have been changed to make them more appropriate worldwide. The species is actually less common in Louisiana than in many other areas.*

The long, sharp bill of the Great Blue Heron (Ardea herodias) has evolved into an effective fish spear. Almost any fish less than a foot in length is potential prey for this common predator.

Less colorful than the breeding adult, this immature Great Blue Heron nevertheless shows the characteristic large bill, long neck and legs, gray plumage, and dark head markings of its species.

*The Yellow-crowned Night-Heron (Nycticorax violaceus) is a crab specialist, stalking the beaches and mud flats for fiddler crabs along the Atlantic, Caribbean, and tropical Pacific coasts.*

Yellow-crowned Night-Herons and most other herons display and mate at their nests. The displaying of the fancy plumes, with accompanying vocalizations, occurs over a lengthy period of courtship.

The beautifully plumaged Bare-throated Tiger-Heron (Tigrisoma mexicanum) hunts for fish and frogs at forested pond and stream edges in Mexico and Central America. Unlike many herons, it is a solitary nester.

Slow and graceful fliers, Great Blue Herons (Ardea herodias) keep their long neck folded back while in the air. They look the size of eagles in flight, because of their very large wings, but they weigh much less than an eagle.

At close range, the Great
Blue Heron (Ardea herodias)
is transformed into a
composition of striking
contrasts: muted colors,
lacy plumes, dagger bill, and
cold, yellow eyes.

*Stork colors can be bright, although most are black and white.*
*The spectacular saddlebill Stork (Ephippiorhynchus senegalensis) is*
*an uncommon but widespread species of African wetlands.*

*Graceful and elegant in flight, the carrion-eating Marabou Stork (Leptoptilus crumeniferus) is no more attractive at close range than the vultures with which it feeds. The function of the huge air sac on the breast is unknown.*

*Yellow-billed Storks (Ibis ibis) feed by touch, moving through the water rapidly with their bill partly open until they come in contact with a fish, frog, or large insect. A gulp and it's gone.*

The Shoebill (Balaeniceps rex) is a very rare relative of the storks. It inhabits the papyrus marshes of central Africa, where it feeds on fishes and frogs, scooping them out of the water with its bizarre bill.

The long, narrow wings of Great Frigatebirds (Fregata minor)—masters of the air—allow them to glide indefinitely. Their bones are so light that their skeleton weighs less than their feather coat!

Male Great Frigatebirds display in groups, with expanded throats and whinnying calls. The females soar above the displaying males, checking them out before finally landing next to the bird of their choice.

*The black wing tips on White Ibises (Eudocimus albus) serve to reduce wear on these vigorously used feathers, allowing them to last from one year's molt to the next. Unlike herons, ibises hold their necks extended in flight.*

*White Ibises lack the plumes of the distantly related herons, but, like them, they nest in trees in colonies, sometimes numbering in the thousands. When displaying, an ibis calls and expands the gular pouch under its bill.*

The long, curved, sensitive bills of White Ibises make excellent probes
for the discovery and capture of small animals in muddy or wet areas.
Their diet includes crabs, crayfish, snails, fish, insects, and even snakes.

*Brightest among the many brightly
pigmented wading birds, the Scarlet
Ibis (Eudocimus ruber) is locally
common in northern South America.
The black bill of this bird indicates
it is ready for breeding.*

*White Ibises (Eudocimus albus) are highly gregarious.
They not only nest in groups but also feed, roost, and
fly in flocks. The brown immatures mix with the white
adults in flocks flying in lines or V formations like geese.*

*Up to 50 male Guianan Cocks-of-the-Rock (Rupicola rupicola)*
*gather in communal display grounds called leks, where*
*they attract females by their loud calls and active displays.*

*Cocks-of-the-Rock are so named because they live in rocky country. The nest is plastered to the side of a cave entrance or vertical rock wall, and the female incubates the two eggs and raises the young by herself.*

*Eye-dazzling at close range, male Andean Cocks-of-the-Rock (Rupicola peruviana) are surpsingly difficult to observe when not in display. The females are much duller in coloration.*

*Males of the Guiananan Cock-of-the-Rock vie with one another for the best display sites, at times even resorting to physical combat. These colorful birds inhabit the rain forests of the Orinoco region.*

*Keas (Nestor notabilis) attract the attention of visitors to New Zealand's mountains by their boldness. Primarily fruit-eaters, they scavenge camp sites and unfortunately are also fond of rubber!*

*Found only in the mountain forests of a single, small
Caribbean island, the beautiful, rare St. Lucia Parrot (Amazona
versicolor) is the subject of an all-out effort to ensure its survival.*

This Hyacinthine Macaw from central Brazil, largest of all parrots, can afford to be conspicuous because it has few natural predators. The pet trade has severely reduced its populations, however.

Flocks of long-tailed Superb Parrots (Polytelis swainsonii) of southeastern Australia can come into conflict with human values when they leave their eucalyptus woodlands to feed on grain crops.

*The Chestnut-fronted Macaw (Ara severa) has the naked face skin and large bill that are characteristic of all macaws. Its relatively small size and the chestnut patch on its forehead distinguish it from the other species.*

Following Page:
*Different species of birds sometimes mate and produce hybrids, both in the wild and in captivity. On the right is a Scarlet Macaw (Ara macao), on the left a hybrid between it and a Blue-and-yellow Macaw (Ara ararauna).*

*Hyacinthine Macaws (Anodorhynchus hyacinthinus) and other large parrots mate for life and are almost invariably seen in pairs, even when in flocks. They lay two white eggs in tree holes.*

*The long tails, bright colors, and loud, raucous cries of Scarlet Macaws (Ara macao) make them an unforgettable symbol of the tropical rain forest as flocks sweep over undisturbed expanses of the Amazon basin.*

*The huge bills of Blue-and-yellow Macaws (Ara ararauna) suit them for cracking the large seeds of many tropical-forest trees. Captive birds have been known to reduce wooden cages to splinters.*

*Just as blue and yellow crayons make green, the green color of Blue-and-yellow Macaws (Ara ararauna) is produced where the yellow pigment of the underparts and the blue-reflecting feathers of the upperparts overlap.*

*Although the yellow of the Blue-and-yellow Macaw is a pigment, the blue is not: it is caused by the microstructure of the feathers reflecting only blue light rays while transmitting all the other wave lengths.*

*Birds have muscular control over every feather in their body, and they can raise them or lower them to warm up or cool off by changing the effectiveness of the insulation provided by the feather coat.*

*Rainbow Lorikeets
(Trichoglossus haematodus)
are nectar-feeding parrots,
using their brush-tipped
tongues to lap up the copious
nectar produced by the
flowers they visit.*

*Shrieking flocks of Rainbow
Lorikeets add color and sound
to any scene. They visit
flowering trees in woodlands
and gardens throughout
eastern and northern Australia.*

*With populations evolved in
isolation, Rainbow Lorikeets
from New Guinea look quite
different from Australian
individuals of the same species.
Nevertheless, they share
the same basic life style.*

*Pairs of Papuan Lorikeets (Charmosyna papou) whir through New Guinea mountain forests in search of flowering trees. Oddly, some individuals at higher elevations have the red color mostly replaced by black.*

*Like many other tropical-forest birds, the Palm Cockatoo (Probosciger aterrimus) has a low reproductive rate, laying only a single egg each year. It is found only in New Guinea and northern Australia.*

*Cockatoo (Cacatua galerita) drops its feet as brakes and spreads wide its wings and tail for maximum support.*

*It is difficult to explain the profligate colors of a bill such as that of the Keel-billed Toucan (Ramphastos sulfuratus), and biologists study such wonders just for a better understanding of nature.*

Their huge bills allow Toco Toucans (Ramphastos toca) to sit quietly
in one place in a fruiting tree and pluck small fruits one after the other.
The bill, full of air pockets, weighs scarcely anything.

*The male Yellow-billed Hornbill (Tockus flavirostris) seals his mate in their nest hole while she incubates, except for a slit through which he feeds her. Both sexes feed the young similarly.*

*Barbets are close relatives of toucans, and the brightly colored Toucan Barbet (Semnornis ramphastinus) may be similar to long-extinct toucan ancestors. The barbet, with a much smaller bill, also eats fruits.*

*Limited to the lower mountain slopes of Colombia and Ecuador, the Crimson-rumped Toucanet (Aulacorhynchus haematopygus) forages for fruits in the cloud-forest canopy with dozens of other fruit-eating species.*

*Smaller than most other toucans, the Blue-throated Toucanet (Aulacorhynchus caeruleogularis) is well-protected from predators by its camouflage. Green is a common color in tropical-forest birds.*

Vulture heads are naked so their feathers won't become matted when feeding on carrion, but the head of the King Vulture (Sarcoramphus papa) is further decorated for display.

Flocks of Red-billed Hornbills (Tockus erythrorhynchus) move through African woodlands, hunting large insects and lizards on the ground or visiting fig trees for a meal of fruit.

*Abyssinian Ground Hornbills, locally common in North Africa, are scavengers and reptile predators. The long, sharp bill is perfect for snatching a lizard or snake in the grass.*

*Rhinoceros Hornbills (Buceros rhinoceros) are superficially similar to toucans—both are fruit-eaters—but are not related to them. This species is restricted to the rain forests of southeast Asia.*

*Quite different from other hornbills, the turkey-sized Abyssinian Ground Hornbill (Bucorvus abyssinicus) flies only to attain its night roost in trees away from terrestrial predators.*

Most trogons are green and well-camouflaged from above, but their red or yellow underparts are conspicuous. The Violaceous Trogon (Trogon violaceus) is common at the forest edge.

*In its orange coloration, this Orange-backed Troupial (Icterus jamacaii) of the Orinoco River exemplifies the many troupials and orioles that occur from Argentina to southern Canada.*

*Male Regent Bowerbirds (Sericulus chrysocephalus) construct a bower with a floor and wall of twigs, deposit brightly colored objects in it, and dance for the brown females they attract.*

*The amazing Hoopoe (Upupa epops) is distasteful to predators, advertising this fact with its vivid wing pattern. Thus it can keep its head down with little danger while digging for buried insects with its long bill.*

*Turacos are African fruit-eating birds with unique red and green pigments; all other bird greens, like blues, are structural. This is a Red-crested Turaco (Tauraco erythrolophus).*

*The male Long-tailed Widowbird (Euplectes progne), one of the longest-tailed birds, hovers over East African grasslands—a black slash on a green landscape—to attract females.*

*Like all green forest birds, the Golden-fronted Leafbird (Chloropsis aurifrons) of Southeast Asia disappears in the foliage, but at close range it is conspicuous to others of its species.*

*Green Barbets (*Megalaima zeylancia*) are well-camouflaged*
*birds of southern Asia that call incessantly from forest treetops.*
*They can best be seen when they gather in fruiting trees.*

*The fruit-doves of southern Asia, Australasia, and Pacific islands are among the gaudiest of birds, brighter even than the colorful fruits they eat. This beautiful fruit-dove is a Beautiful Fruit-Dove (Ptilinopus pulchellus).*

*The gorgeous Elegant Trogon (Trogon elegans) of Mexico, the only trogon to breed in the United States, attracts hundreds of birdwatchers to the pine-oak woodlands of southern Arizona every summer.*

*The huge bill of the Spangled Kookaburra (Dacelo tyro) from New Guinea—a relative of the Laughing Kookaburra of Australia—fits it for its diet of large insects, lizards, and even small mammals.*

*A common fruit-eating forest-canopy bird of Southeast Asia, the male Asian Fairy Bluebird (Irena puella) is unmistakable. The female, a much duller blue-green all over, is well camouflaged.*

Tanagers are among the most common and most
colorful birds of the New World tropics. The Speckled
(Tangara guttata) and Bay-headed (Tangara gyrola)
Tanagers shown here are closely related.

The Golden-fronted Leafbird
(Chloropsis aurifrons) is a
common bird throughout
Southeast Asia. Accomplished
singers, males also mimic the songs
and calls of many other species.

*Female Resplendent Quetzals (Pharomachrus mocinno) are much less brightly colored than the males, which are brilliantly green-backed and red-bellied like other trogons. This species is the national bird of Guatemala.*

*Black-throated Trogons (Trogon rufus) perch quietly for long periods, flutter up to pull off a fruit or capture a large insect, then often return to the same perch to eat it.*

*Visiting a hibiscus flower even before it opens, this Red-tailed Comet (*Sappho sparganura*) samples its nectar by piercing it at its base. Almost all hummingbirds hover to feed.*

*Carmine Bee-eaters (Merops nubicus) are noteworthy not only for their incandescent colors but also for their habit of perching on large animals that flush insects for them.*

*A familiar sight over much of South and East African wooded plains, the Lilac-breasted Roller (Coracias caudata) has a breathtaking aerial display flight, in which it rolls and tumbles while diving through the air.*

Common in the mountains of Bolivia and Argentina, the Red-tailed Comet (Sappho sparganura) is one of the most spectacular of the 320 species of hummingbirds. All are restricted to the Americas.

All hummingbirds have long, slender bills and tubular tongues for nectar-feeding, although few have tails so magnificent as this Violet-tailed Sylph (Aglaiocercus coelestis) of Colombia and Ecuador.

Flocks of European Bee-eaters (Merops apiaster) are prominent among the millions of migrants that fly between breeding grounds in Europe and wintering grounds in Africa.

Cinnamon-chested Bee-eaters (Merops oreobates) nest in small groups in holes in sand banks in the mountains of East Africa. At some nests, additional "helpers" of the same species assist in feeding the young.

The Indian Roller (Coracias benghalensis) of southern Asia shows the bright wing markings that make some species so conspicuous in flight for territorial or courtship display.

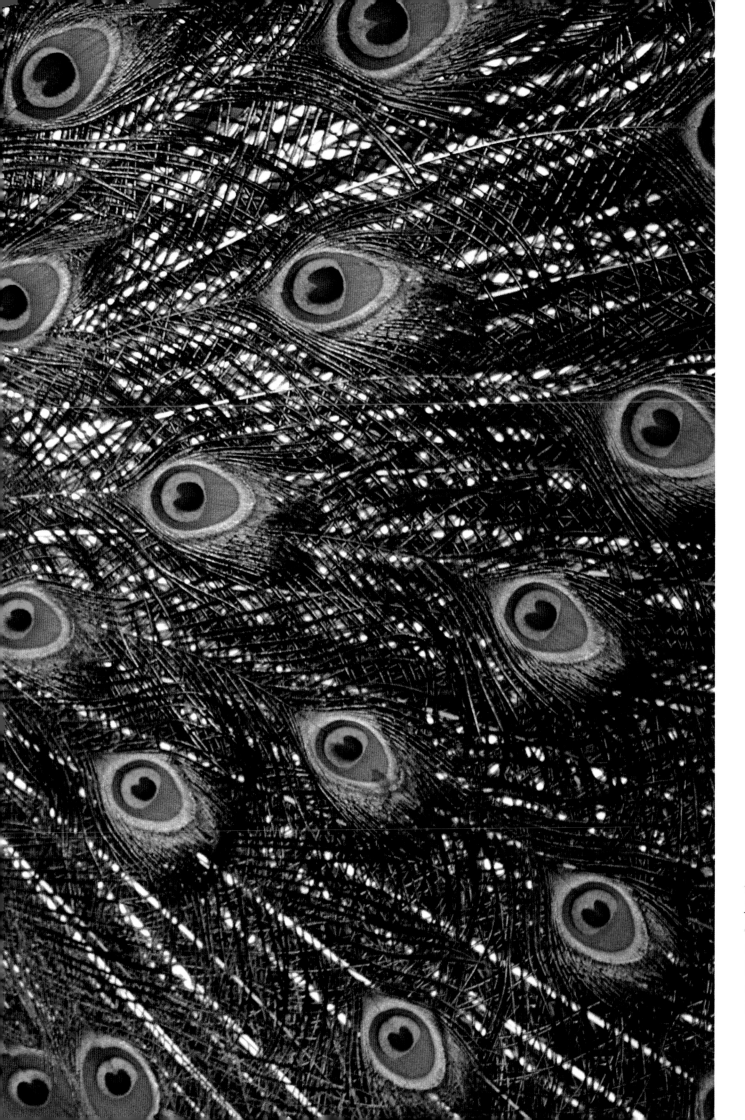

The "tail" of the male Blue Peafowl (Pavo cristatus) is actually its uppertail coverts—200 of them—lengthened and spangled to create one of the most impressive of bird displays.

Small flocks of Blue Peafowls (Pavo cristatus), like huge chickens, scratch for seeds, fruits, and insects at roadsides in their native India. Their loud calls resound through the countryside at dawn and dusk.

Male Blue Peafowls must virtually lack predators to have evolved such conspicuous plumage and a "tail" large enough to make flight awkward. The females are mostly brown, without the accoutrements of the males.

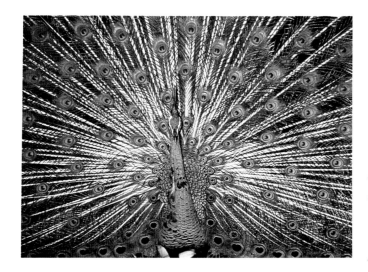

Less familiar although no less spectacular than its blue relative, the Green Peafowl (Pavo muticus) replaces it in lowland forests farther east, from eastern India to Vietnam.

The overall appearance of a bird such as this male Blue Peafowl (Pavo cristatus) comes from the exquisite details of the patterning of its individual feathers. In this species the effect is dazzling.

*Albinism is possible in any bird, but domesticated birds such as pigeons, chickens, ducks, and others have been bred for white color. It seems a loss in the case of the peacock.*

*The huge Victoria Crowned Pigeons (Goura victoria) inhabit the lowland rain forests of New Guinea, where they forage for fruit that has fallen from the trees. They differ from the other crowned pigeons by their crest color.*

*As in other pigeons, Western Crowned Pigeons (*Goura cristata*) make untidy stick nests, in which they lay one or two eggs. Both sexes feed the young with "pigeon's milk," produced in their crop.*

*Golden Pheasants (Chrysolophus pictus) inhabit mountain forests of southern China and are rarely seen, except in winter, when they emerge to feed in fields and gardens. Fortunate indeed is such a gardener.*

*Although familiar because it has been introduced widely in the temperate regions of the world as a game species, the male Ring-necked Pheasant (Phasianus colchicus) is no less beautiful than many a rarer bird.*

The male Australian Brush-turkey (Alectura lathami) gathers dead leaves together into a large mound, in which the female lays her eggs. The heat from the decaying leaves incubates the eggs.

Like many other brightly colored forest birds, the Blyth's Tragopan (Tragopan blythi) is difficult to see where it occurs in the dense rhododendron and bamboo thickets of the eastern Himalayas.

Southern Screamers (Chauna torquata), looking like chickens but related to ducks and geese, are common around southern South American marshes. They are aptly named, with the loudest calls of any bird of the pampas.

The spectacular plumage decorations of birds such as this Blue-eared Pheasant are most impressive at close range. Naked skin colors are often emphasized in this group of birds.

Temperate forests and meadows of central China are the home of the Blue-eared Pheasant (Crossoptilon auritum), unusual among pheasants in that both sexes look alike.

*The bills of pheasants such as this Chinese Tragopan (*Tragopan caboti*), like their chicken relatives, are rather generalized: adapted for taking both seeds and insects from the ground.*

*Male Great Argus Pheasants (*Argusianus argus*) clear debris and vegetation away from a large area on the forest floor, where they perform spectacular displays with opened wings and tail.*

The Crimson Tragopan of the Himalayan forests is quite shy, appropriate for a bird so likely to catch the eye of a predator. Females, which incubate the eggs and must be camouflaged, are brown and streaked.

As if the brilliant plumage were not enough, the male Crimson Tragopan (Tragopan satyra) extends an ornately marked throat lappet in display. It counfounds human observers to see females seemingly ignore such a display.

*The striking white wing patches of Gray Crowned Cranes (Balearica regulorum) in flight are a signal of their presence to all other cranes in the area, as are their loud, bugling calls.*

*The velvety front and hairlike rear of the crown
of this Black Crowned Crane (Balearica pavonina)
of West and North Africa shows how much the
feathers may be modified for display.*

*Males and females of most water birds, for example, these Gray Crowned Cranes,
look alike and are probably distinguished by their behavior.
This species is restricted to East and South Africa.*

*Mated Japanese and other cranes "dance" even during their winter sojourn, this courtship behavior serving to maintain their pair bond through the year. The naked red head skin, a source of heat loss, shrinks during the winter.*

*Young Japanese Cranes (Grus japonensis), distinguished from their parents by their brown heads, accompany them on their wintering grounds. However, in most groups of birds, the adults and young migrate separately.*

*White-naped Cranes (Grus vipio) breed in eastern Siberia and winter very locally in Korea, southern Japan, and northeastern China. Subject to human disturbance, most cranes have declined in numbers in historic times.*

*The very large Sarus Crane (Grus antigone) stands as tall as a person. This species inhabits the freshwater marshes of southern Asia, each pair raising the two young during the long rainy season.*

*With its long bill, the Wattled crane (Bugeranus carunculatus) of Africa digs in the soil for grass seeds and insects, but it also feeds from the ground surface as do most other cranes.*

*Japanese Cranes (Grus japonensis) mate for life and are revered in Japan as symbols of love and marital fidelity, as well as long life. They breed locally in marshes and grasslands of Siberia as well as northern Japan.*

99

*The American Avocet (Recurvirostra americana) is a long-legged shorebird that breeds at saline lakes of western North America. Like a spoonbill, it feeds by sweeping its bill through the water to capture small crustaceans.*

*Although they look awkward in them, Roseate Spoonbills (Ajaia ajaja) and other long-legged wading birds are adapted to perch in trees, which provide both nesting and roosting sites.*

The Roseate Spoonbill's "spoon" allows
it to capture large numbers of small,
shrimplike animals by sweeping its bill
rapidly back and forth in shallow water.
The immature has a feathered head,
the adult a naked head.

The conspicuous coloration of Roseate Spoonbills and many
other water birds allows them to find one another readily as
they fly long distances between roosting and feeding sites.

*The bill of the Roseate Spoonbill, although specialized and awkward looking, is perfectly effective for preening, gathering nesting material, and pecking territorial intruders, as well as feeding.*

*Roseate Spoonbills and other wading birds often roost in shallow water, where they are safe from land-based predators and such as bobcats and foxes and aquatic predators such as crocodilians.*

*Also called Snakebird and Water Turkey because of its long neck
and tail, the common name Anhinga and the scientific name
Anhinga anhinga come from the Tupi Indian language of Brazil.*

*It is appropriate for birds to be curious about the other animals of their environment, but one wonders what this Anhinga is thinking as it looks over a Florida Red-bellied Turtle at an Everglades waterhole.*

*Anhingas swim slowly beneath the water's surface, capture high-bodied fish by spearing them with the slender, pointed bill, and bring them to the surface to be swallowed. The expansible throat makes this feat possible.*

*The ribbing on the tails of both female (brown neck) and male (black neck) Anhingas may be for display, but no one knows for sure. Often individual biologists become intrigued by such problems and proceed to solve them.*

*The Brown-hooded Kingfisher (Halcyon albiventris) watches for grasshoppers and other insects from an exposed perch in open African woodlands. The nest is placed in a hole in an earth bank.*

*Eurasian Kingfishers (Alcedo atthis) are very wide-ranging, furnishing bright spots of streamside color from the British Isles all the way across to Japan and down to New Guinea.*

*Very diffrently colored from its drab rail relatives, the Purple Gallinule (Porphyula martinica) flaunts its dazzling colors in the open in tropical American marshes. The long toes allow it to walk on lily pads.*

*Making up in bill what it lacks in body, the sparrow-sized Malachite Kingfisher (Alcedo cristata) captures fish almost as long as itself from African streams and pools.*

*Almost restricted to New Guinea, birds of paradise are among nature's most glorious creatures. They are closely related to crows, but there the similarity ends, as is apparent in this male Greater Bird of Paradise (Paradisea apoda) in display.*

*Reddish Egrets (Egretta rufescens) come in two colors, reddish or white, independent of sex and age. The two types, which freely mate with one another, are similar in every way but color.*

*The eye color of birds is important in display and species recognition just as is the coloration of the feathers. The Reddish Egret has white eyes, but the eyes of other herons are yellow, red, brown, or gray.*

*Reddish Egrets forage by dashing around the shallows with quick changes of direction, pursuing fish in a way that looks ludicrous. Nevertheless, this technique is just as effective as the patient stalking method of other species.*

Reddish Egrets are restricted to salt water, and they can be seen giving their striking courtship display at breeding colonies on the shores of the Caribbean and the Gulf Coast of the United States.

*The broad wings of herons and egrets, such as this Great Egret (Casmerodius albus), allow them to fly slowly in search of feeding places and land gently on their long, delicate legs.*

*Unlike the other egrets that share mixed breeding assemblages, the Great Egret lacks head plumes. Structures such as these, as well as bill color, give a very different appearance to each of the egret species.*

The lacy plumes of the Great Egrets and other herons grow during the breeding season to indicate maturity and readiness to mate. They grow quickly, as they are not complexly constructed for insulation like most feathers.

111

*Great Egrets typically lay three eggs but often fledge only two young. In times of food shortage, larger (older) young are quite aggressive toward smaller young, taking from them and, at times, killing them.*

*At the beginning of the breeding season, Great Egret (Casmerodius albus) colonies present scenes of constant activity, with pairs courting, keeping neighboring pairs from their small territory, and bringing nest material.*

*Birds cannot lose heat as humans do by perspiring, but on hot days they open their mouths and flutter their throats to cool off. In this way internal moisture evaporates.*

*Although adult Lesser Flamingos (Phoeniconaias minor) are
relatively safe from predators in their open, wet environment, they fly
readily when approached, running until they reach takeoff speed.*

*The extremely long neck and legs are apparent in flying Eurasian Flamingos (Phoenicopterus roseus). Most flamingos are brightest on the wings, making them especially striking in flight.*

*Flamingos collect in tremendous flocks at the Rift Valley lakes of Africa.
These are adult and young Lesser Flamingos (Phoeniconaias minor) and a
Eurasian White Pelican (Pelecanus onocrotalus) at Lake Nakuru.*

*Like all flamingos, the American Flamingo (Phoenicopterus ruber) feeds by striding through the water with its bill upside down, straining out the small crustaceans that form a virtual soup in shallow estuaries.*

*This American Flamingo (Phoenicopterus ruber) shows its peculiar bill, adapted for upside-down feeding, with the plates for straining microorganisms just visible.*

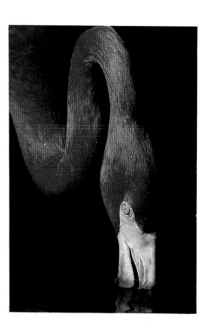

*The American Flamingo pumps water through its specialized straining apparatus with its tongue, constantly swallowing the prey animals that adhere to the bill.*

*Sleeping birds are quite aware of their environment, opening their eyes at any slight sound and ready to spring into flight in a split second. Birds in captivity, where many flamingos are photographed, become more relaxed.*

*Much the brightest of its group, the American Flamingo is locally distributed around the Caribbean and on the coast of northern South America, as well as in the Galápagos Islands.*

*The plumes of Great Egrets (Casmerodius albus) and other egrets almost cost them their existence, as they were hunted on a grand scale at the turn of the century for decorations on women's hats. They are now protected.*

*Of seven species of cranes recorded from Japan, only the Japanese Crane (Grus japonensis) is resident. Pairs and their young join flocks during the winter, often moving to large sanctuaries set aside for them.*

*Each group of differently colored feathers in the gaudy male Golden Pheasant (*Chrysolophus pictus*) is unique not only in coloration but also in feather structure.*

*The white of the egret in the bright sun's light slowly turns to the black of the night, another of the cycles that control the life of every one of the 9,000 species of birds that enrich our planet.*

*Following Page:*
*The Earth will remain a good home for us as long as we assure the survival of all the creatures with which we share it, and there is no better way to make this point than to envision a world without birds.*

*Peacocks face each other or the
peahens when they display, and all
the show is from the front. The true tail
is a supporting actor, as it were, holding
up those magnificent uppertail coverts.*

*The last heron of the day tries for one more fish,
to go to roost a tiny bit ahead of the game.
Tomorrow will be another day in the bird's life:
finding enough food, avoiding predators, and
going about the business of survival.*